# Nature's Cycles
# Seasons

## Dana Meachen Rau

Marshall Cavendish
Benchmark
New York

2

The year has four seasons: spring, summer, fall, and winter. You do different things in each season. Nature changes in each season, too.

In spring, the air is warm.
You can put away your hats
and mittens. But you might
need an umbrella!

Rainwater soaks into the ground. Seeds *sprout*. The new plants begin to grow up toward the sun.

Some animals wake up.
They have slept all winter.
Others animals return home.
They have been in places
where it was warm. Animals
start looking for food. Birds
begin to build nests.

Some animals have babies in spring. Deer have fawns.

Wolves have cubs. Mothers feed
their babies to help them grow.

In summer, the air is hot.
You have lots of time to play
outside. The days are long.
The nights are short.

The sun rises early and sets late. The sun is high in the sky in the middle of the day.

Summer storms can bring lightning and thunder. Dark clouds send rain.

Plants use the water to grow
big and strong. Flowers bloom
in many colors.

Animals can find food easily in summer. They drink water from ponds and creeks.

Some cool off in puddles.
You might cool off from the
hot sun in a puddle, too!

16

In fall, the air is cool. Some plants die. Some leaves change color and fall to the ground. You might need to help rake them up.

Animals get ready for winter by storing food. They also search for *shelter*. A chipmunk may find a *hollow* log.

Frogs dig in mud under the water. A good shelter will keep them warm and safe when winter comes.

Some birds *migrate* to warmer places in the fall. They fly in *flocks* together. They stop to rest and eat.

In winter, the air is cold. The days are short. The nights are long. The sun rises late and sets early. The sun is low in the sky. In some places, snow falls on the ground.

You can put on a warm coat to play outside.

Some animals grow a warmer coat, too. They search for food in the snow.

Other animals *hibernate*. They sleep all winter. Some animals just rest and eat the food they stored.

Many plants are *dormant* in winter. They are still alive, but they do not grow.

Living things wait for spring to come. Nature will change again.

## Challenge Words

**dormant (DOR-mehnt)**—Resting and not growing.

**flocks**—Groups of birds flying together.

**hibernate (HI-buhr-nate)**—To sleep all winter.

**hollow (HAHL-oh)**—Empty in the middle.

**migrate (MY-grate)**—To travel to warmer places.

**shelter**—A safe place to live.

**sprout (sprowt)**—To begin to grow.

# Index

Page numbers in **boldface** are illustrations.

*The author would like to thank Paula Meachen*
*for her scientific guidance and expertise in reviewing this book.*

## With thanks to Nanci Vargus, Ed.D.,
## and Beth Walker Gambro, reading consultants

Marshall Cavendish Benchmark
99 White Plains Road
Tarrytown, New York 10591-9001
www.marshallcavendish.us

Text copyright © 2010 by Marshall Cavendish Corporation

Library of Congress Cataloging-in-Publication Data

Rau, Dana Meachen, 1971–
Seasons / by Dana Meachen Rau.
p. cm. — (Bookworms. Nature's cycles)
Includes index.
Summary: "Introduces the idea that many things in the world around us
are cyclical in nature and discusses how the seasons change"—Provided by publisher.
ISBN 978-0-7614-4098-7
1. Seasons—Juvenile literature. I. Title.
QB637.4.R38 2009
508.2—dc22
2008042507

Editor: Christina Gardeski
Publisher: Michelle Bisson
Designer: Virginia Pope
Art Director: Anahid Hamparian

Photo Research by Anne Burns Images

Cover Photo by *Corbis*/Grafton Smith

The photographs in this book are used with permission and through the courtesy of:
*Corbis*: pp. 1, 16 Robert Llewellyn; p. 8 Tom Brakefield; p. 10 Rolf Bruderer; p. 23 Jorma Jamsen/zefa;
p. 28 Darrell Gulin. *Getty Images*: p. 2 Lori Adamski Peek; p. 13 Steve Satushek; p. 15 Juan Silva;
p. 24 Toshi Kawano. *Photo Edit*: p. 4 Bob Daemmrich. *Peter Arnold, Inc.*: p. 5 C. Huetter;
p. 7 PHONE Cordier Sylvain; p. 9 BIOS/J. Klein & M. Hubert; p. 11 R. Frank; p. 14 Patrick Frischknecht;
p. 18 Ed Reschke; p. 20 Johann Schumacher; p. 25 S. J. Krasemann; p. 27 WILDLIFE.
*Photo Researchers*: p. 12 Kent Wood ; p. 19 Karl H. Switak.

Printed in Malaysia
1  3  5  6  4  2